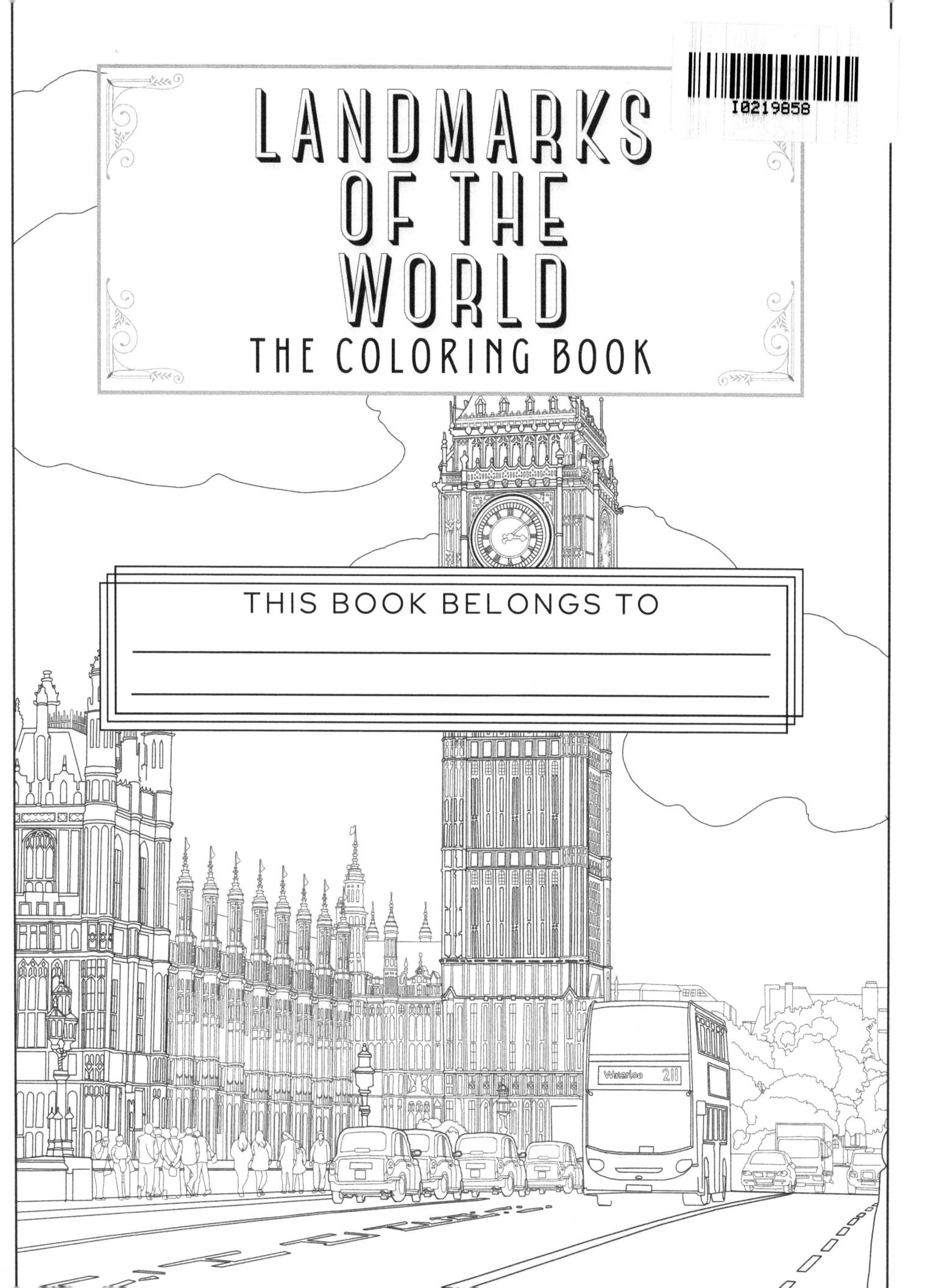

A MESSAGE FROM THE PUBLISHER

Hey, thank you for making the purchase, we really hope you enjoy this book. If you have the chance, then all feedback is greatly appreciated. We have put a lot of effort into making this book, so if you are not completely satisfied, please email us at ben@bclesterbooks.com and we will do our best to address any issues. If you have any suggestions, enquiries or want to send us a selfie with this book, then email at the same address - ben@bclesterbooks.com

Is this book misprinted? Send us an email at ben@bclesterbooks.com with a photo of the misprint and we will send out another copy!

WHO IS B.C. LESTER BOOKS?

B.C. Lester Books is a small publishing firm of three people based in Buckinghamshire, UK. We aim to provide quality works in all things geography, for kids and adults, with varying interests. We have already released a selection of activity, trivia and fact books and are working hard to bring you wider selection. Have a suggestion for us? Then email ben@bclesterbooks.com. We are all ears!

IF YOU ENJOYED THIS COLORING EXPERIENCE, THEN YOU MAY LIKE:

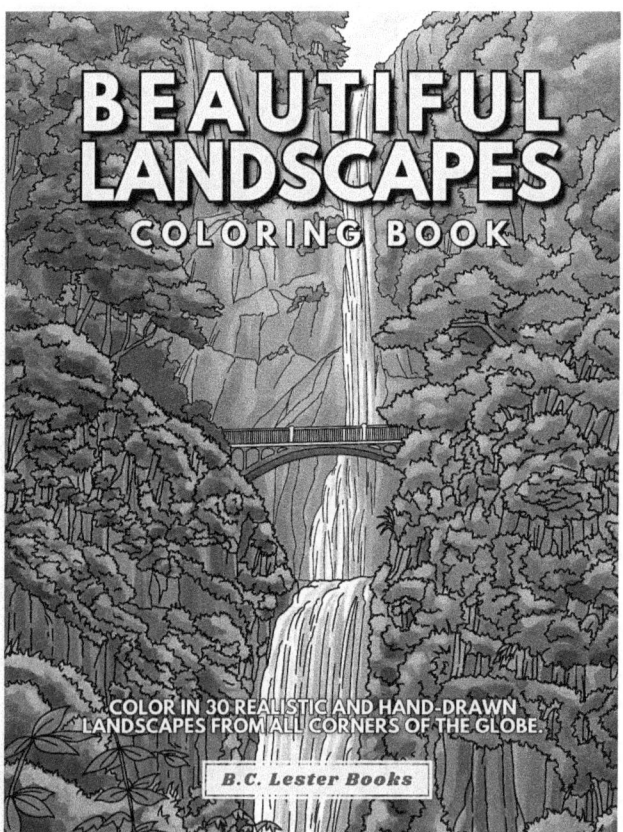

ISBN-10: 1913668401
Unwind, relax, and bring some of our planet's most beautiful natural scenery to life with color!

LANDMARK LOCATIONS

AFRICA & MIDDLE EAST
BURJ AL ARAB 25
BURJ KHALIFA 19
GREAT PYRAMIDS OF GIZA 5
MECCA 9

AMERICAS
CHICHEN ITZA 29
CHRIST REDEEMER 14
EMPIRE STATE BUILDING 22
GOLDEN GATE BRIDGE 17
STATUE OF LIBERTY 7

ASIA PACIFIC
ANGKOR WAT 10
EASTER ISLAND 26
GINKAKU JI 28
MARINA BAY SANDS 20
ORIENTAL PEARL TOWER 12
PETRONAS TOWERS 6
SYDNEY OPERA HOUSE 3
TAJ MAHAL 16

EUROPE
ACROPOLIS 30
ARC DE TRIOMPHE 18
BIG BEN 1
BRANDENBURG GATE 11
COLOSSEUM 8
EIFFEL TOWER 2
LEANING TOWER OF PISA 13
LONDON EYE 21
LOUVRE 23
SAGRADA FAMILIA 4
ST. BASILS CATHEDRAL 15
ST. PETERS BASILICA 24
TOWER BRIDGE 27

B.C. Lester Books
Geography publications for the people since 2019.

Visit us at www.bclesterbooks.com for more!

No part of this book may be copied, reproduced or sold without the express permission from the copyright owner.

Copyright B.C. Lester Books 2021. All rights reserved.

BEFORE YOU START...

Test your coloring equipment here for bleedthrough. **Please note** that this coloring book is NOT recommended for paint, gel pens or highlighters...

READY TO START?
Relax, unwind, and enjoy the experience!

B.C. Lester Books

ELIZABETH TOWER A.K.A 'BIG BEN'

SYDNEY OPERA HOUSE

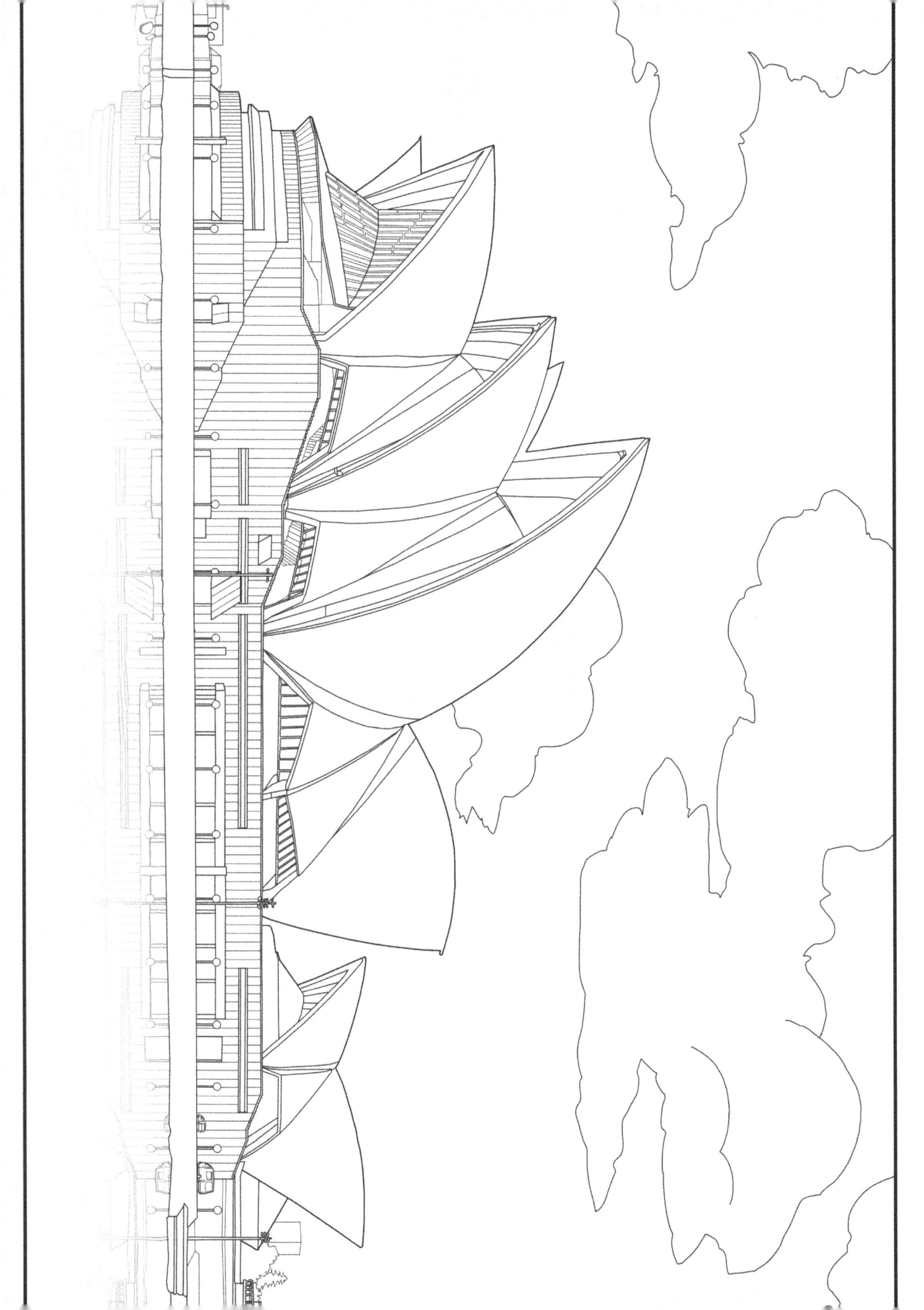

SAGRADA FAMILIA

GREAT PYRAMID OF GIZA

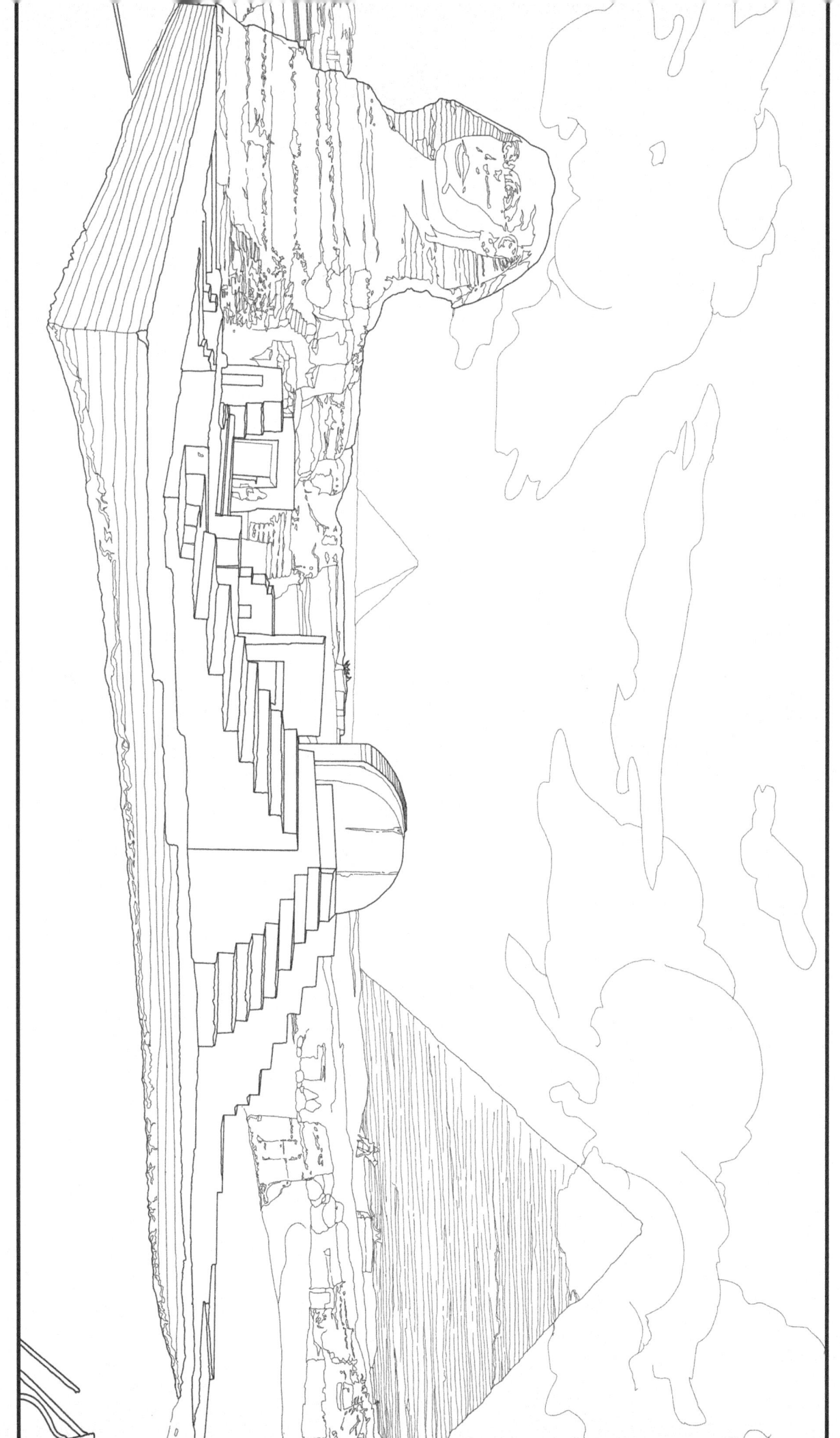

PETRONAS TOWERS

STATUE OF LIBERTY

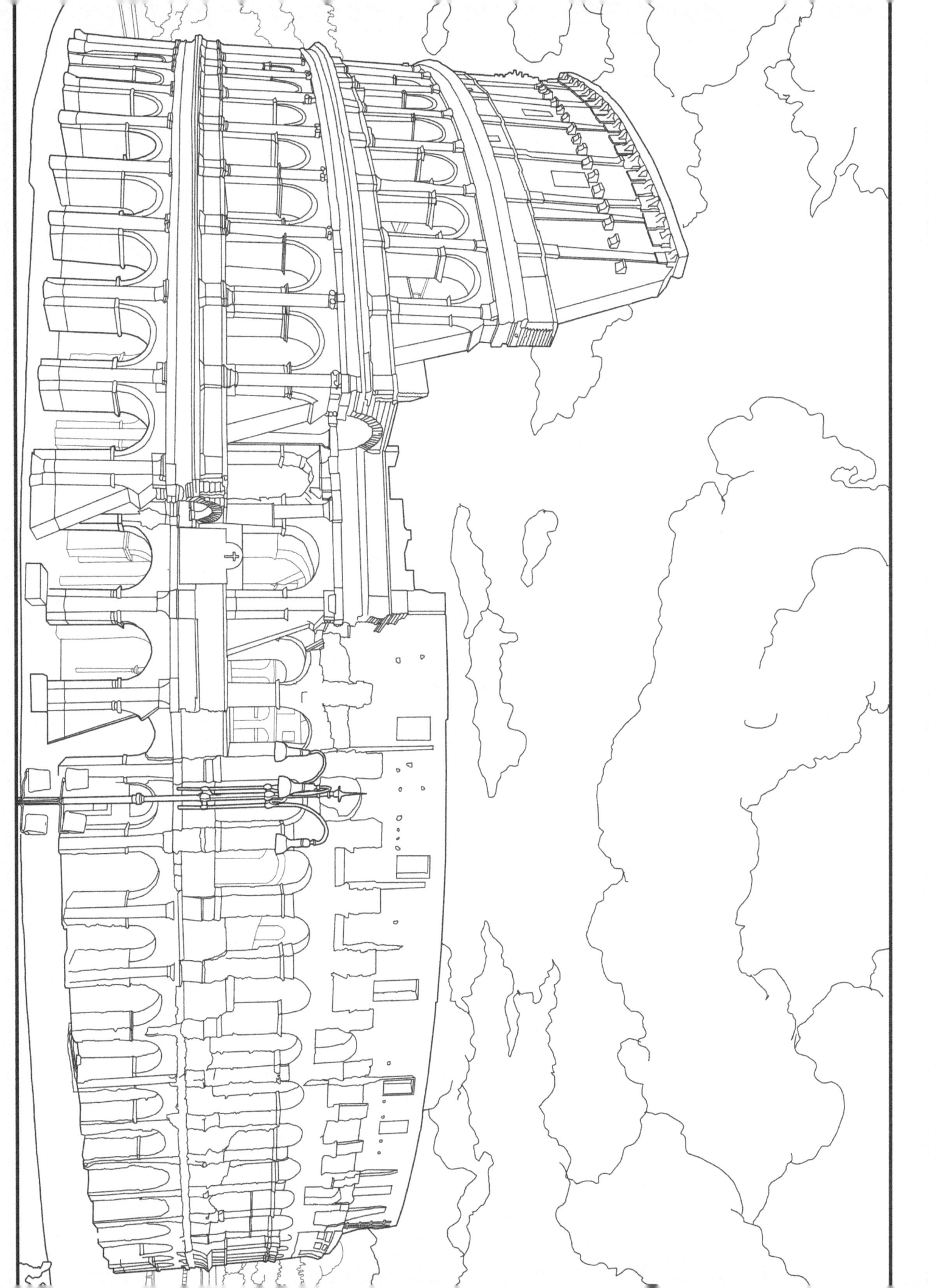

ANGKOR WAT

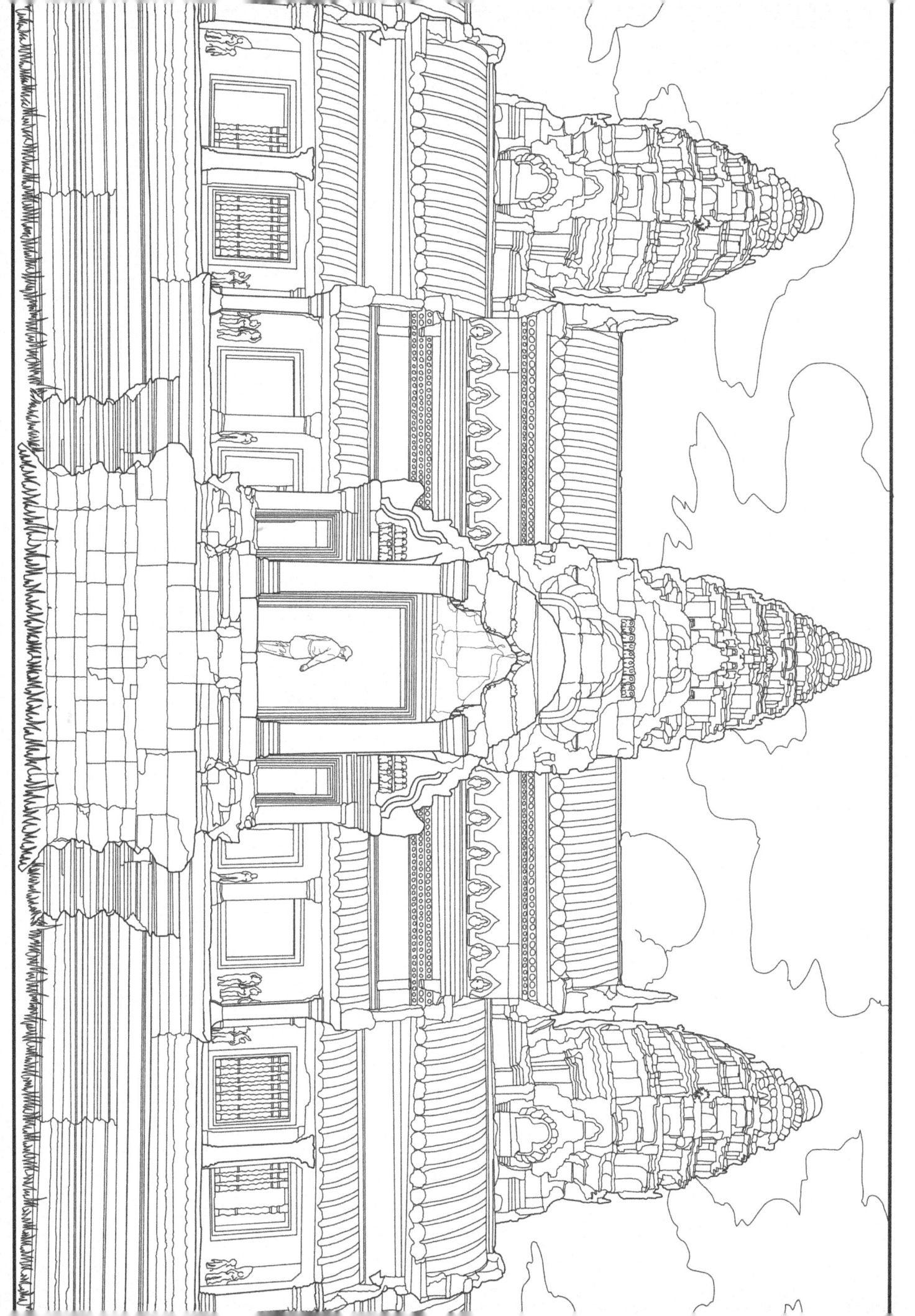

BRANDENBURG GATE

「ORIENTAL PEARL TOWER」

LEANING TOWER OF PISA

CHRIST THE REDEEMER

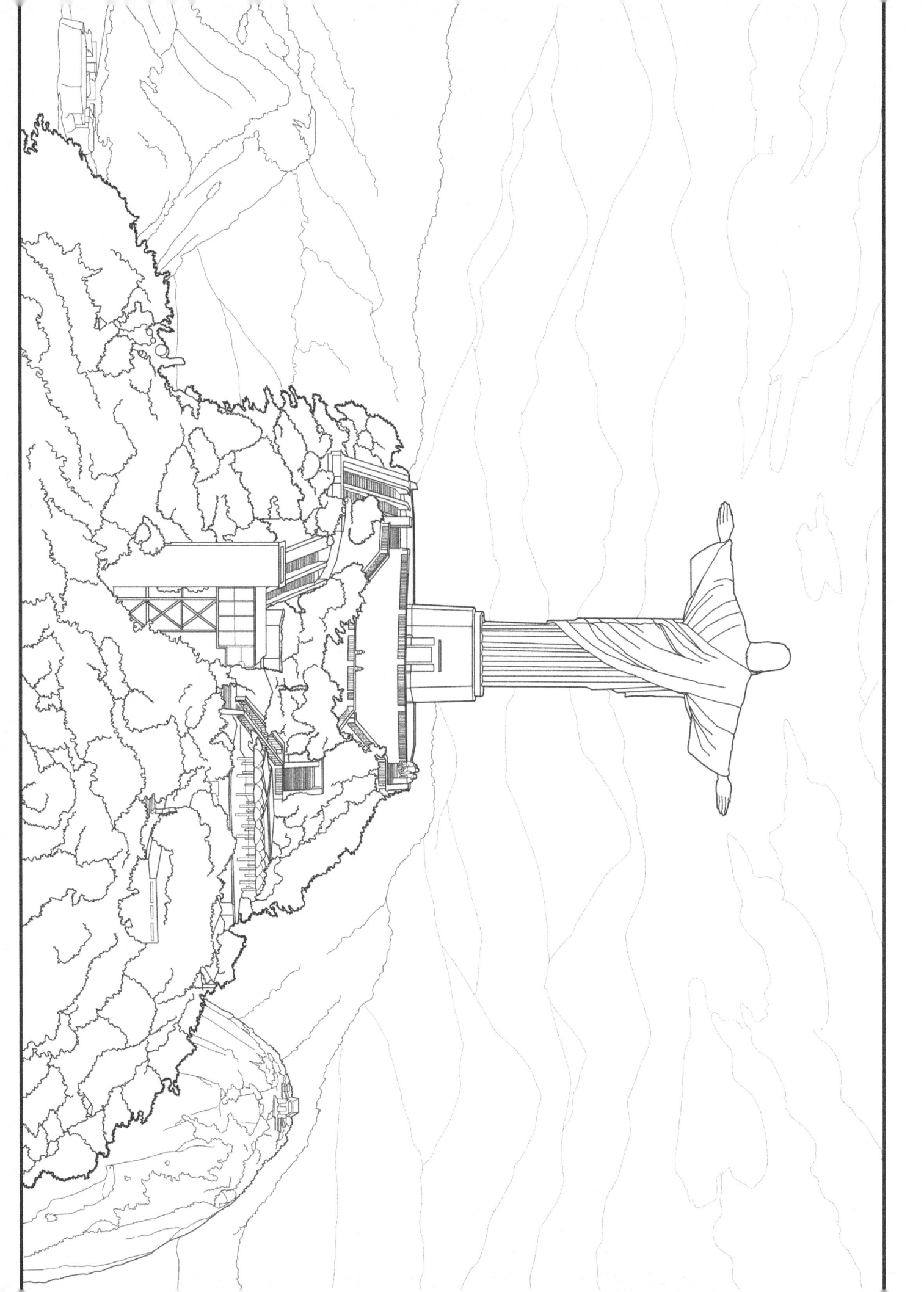

ST. BASIL'S CATHEDRAL

GOLDEN GATE BRIDGE

BURJ KHALIFA

ARC DE TRIOMPHE

MARINA BAY SANDS

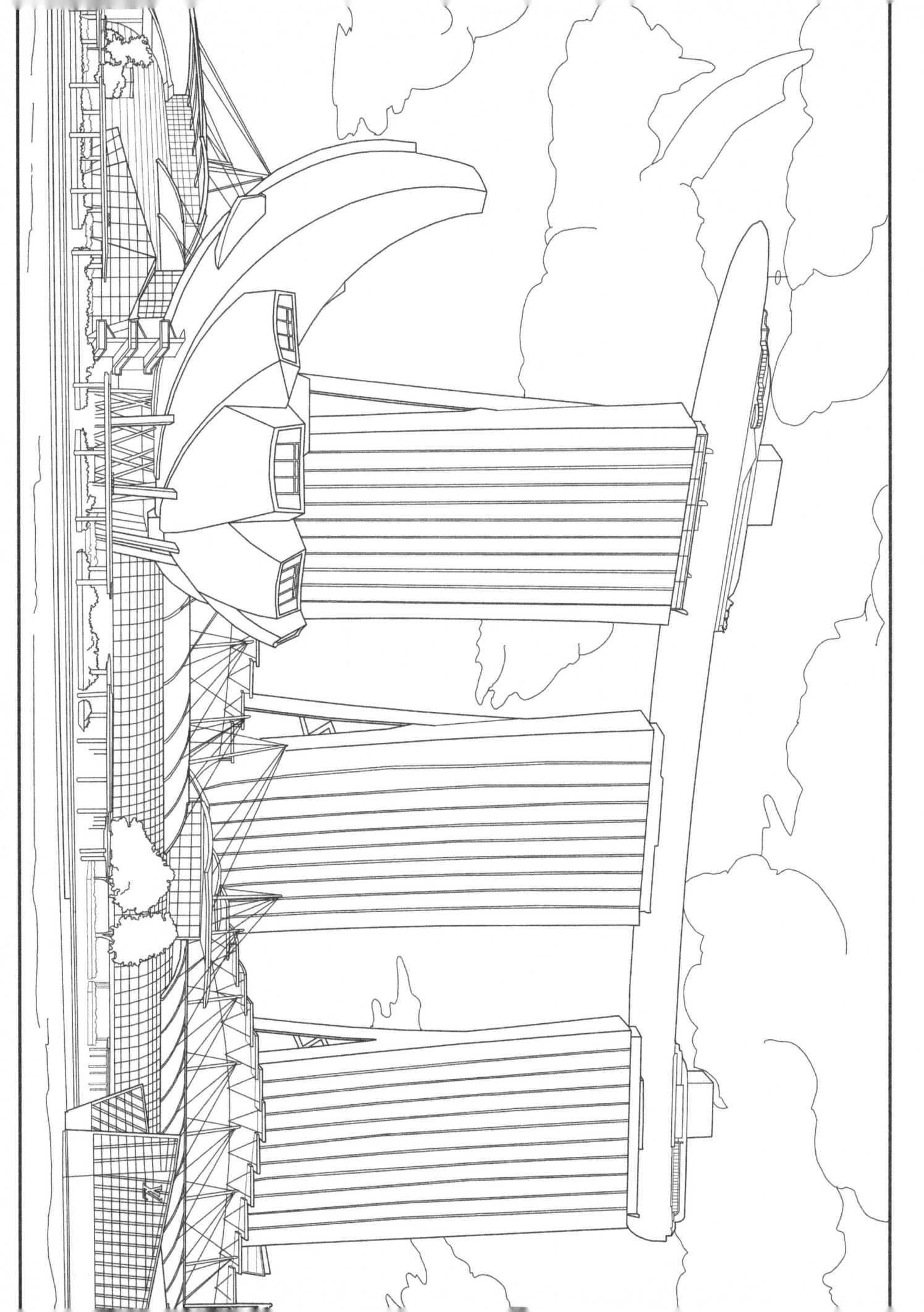

LONDON EYE

EMPIRE STATE BUILDING

LOUVRE

ST. PETER'S BASILICA

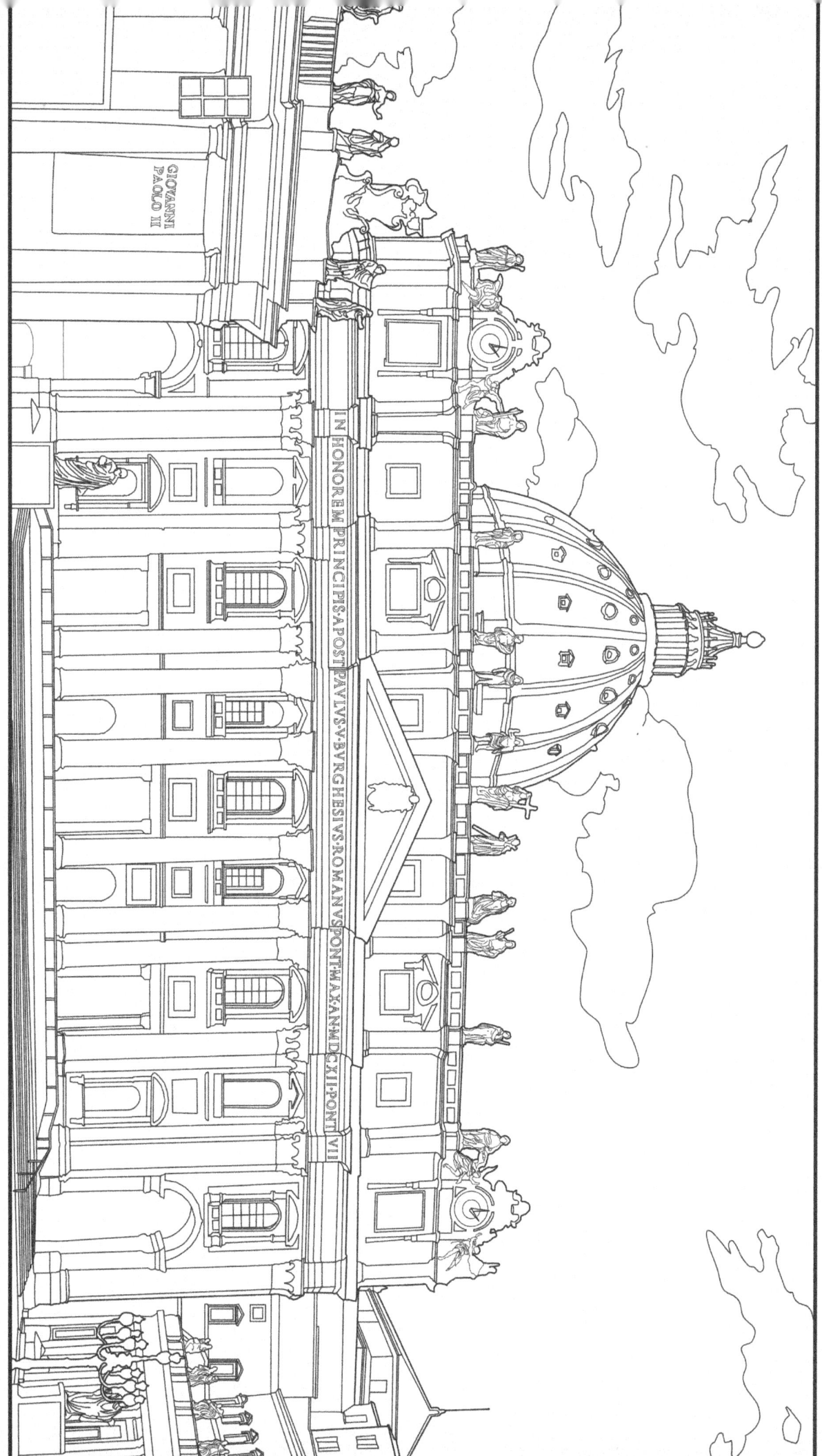

BURJ AL ARAB

26

MOAI OF EASTER ISLAND

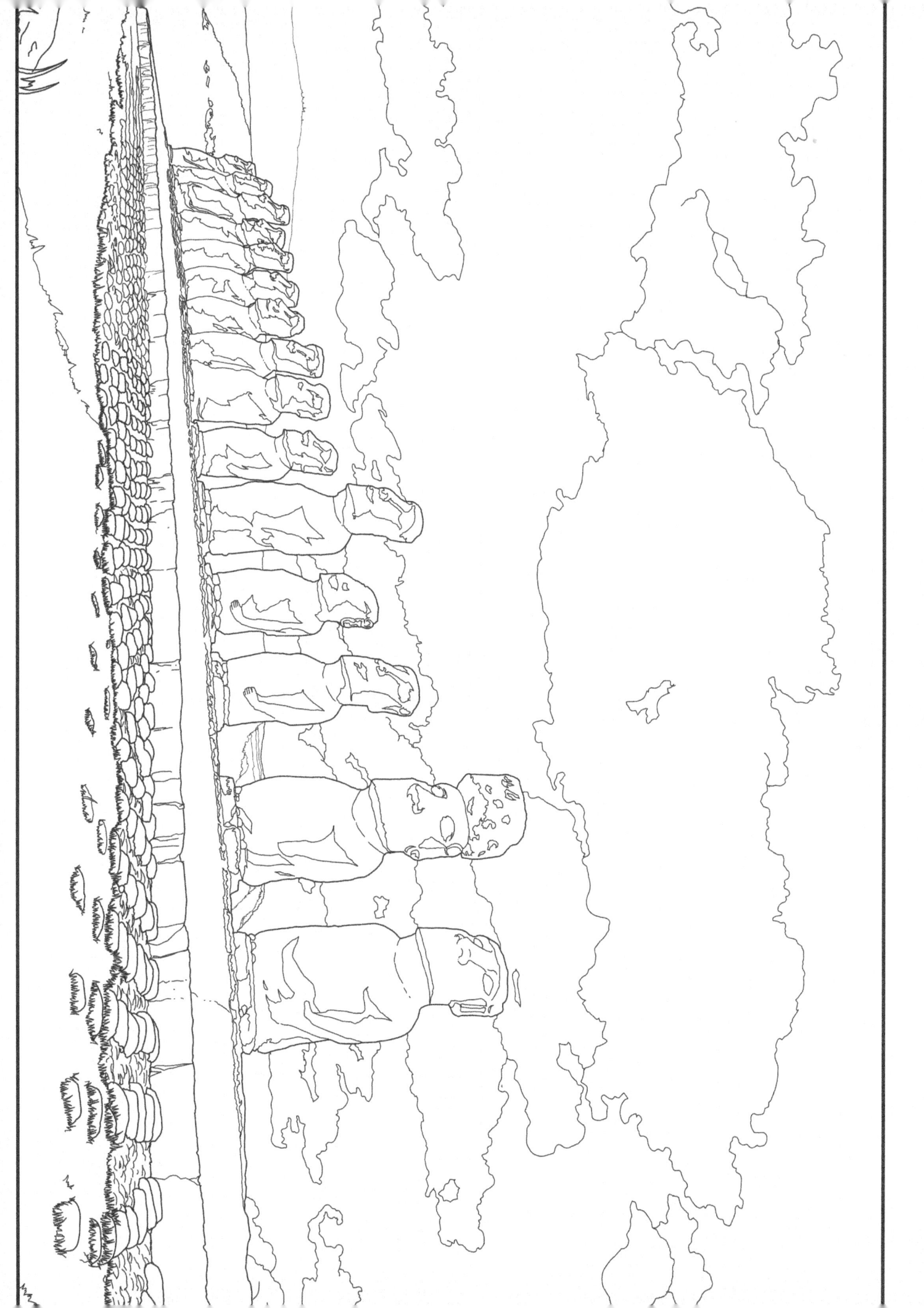

TOWER BRIDGE

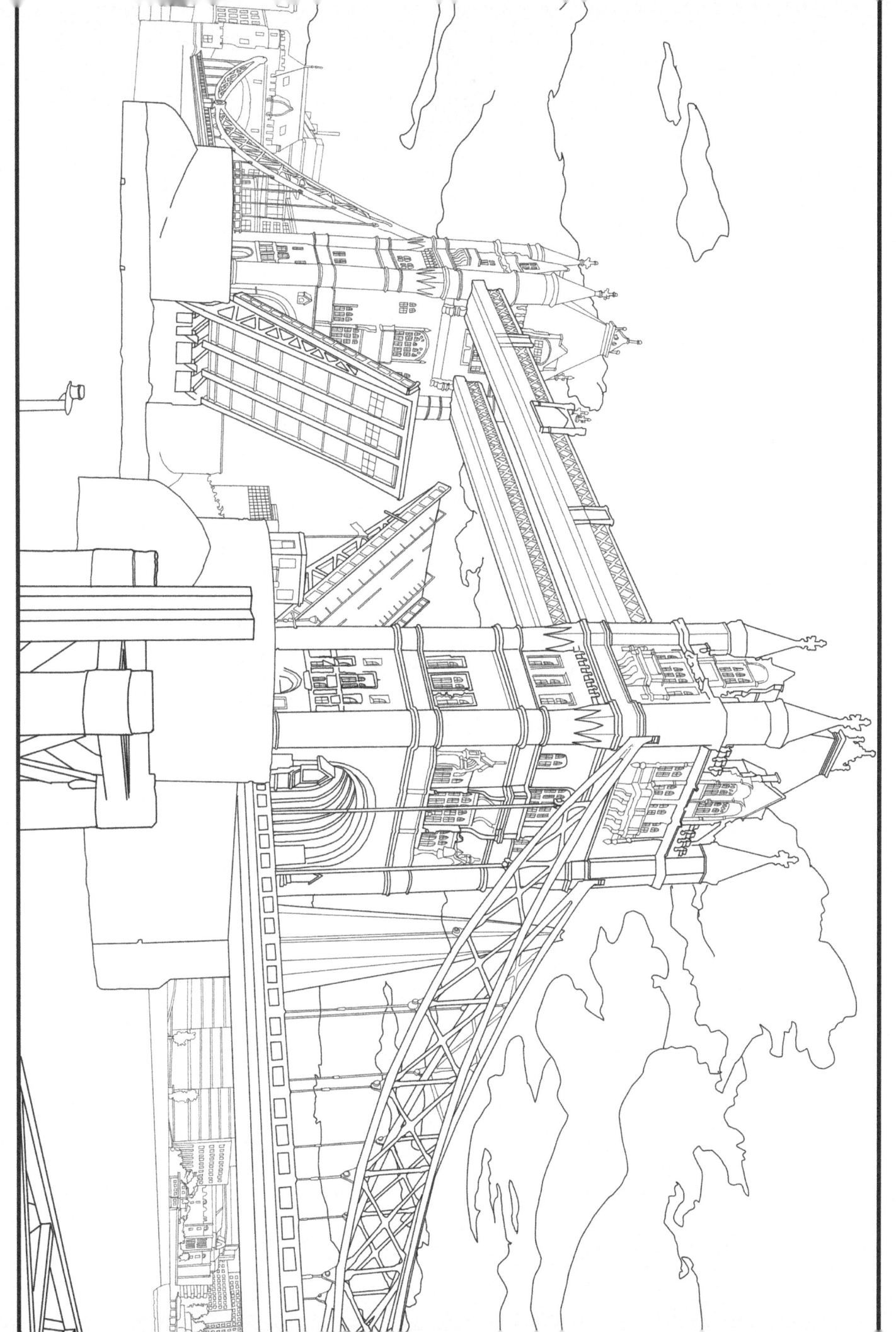

GINKAKU-JI

CHICHEN ITZA

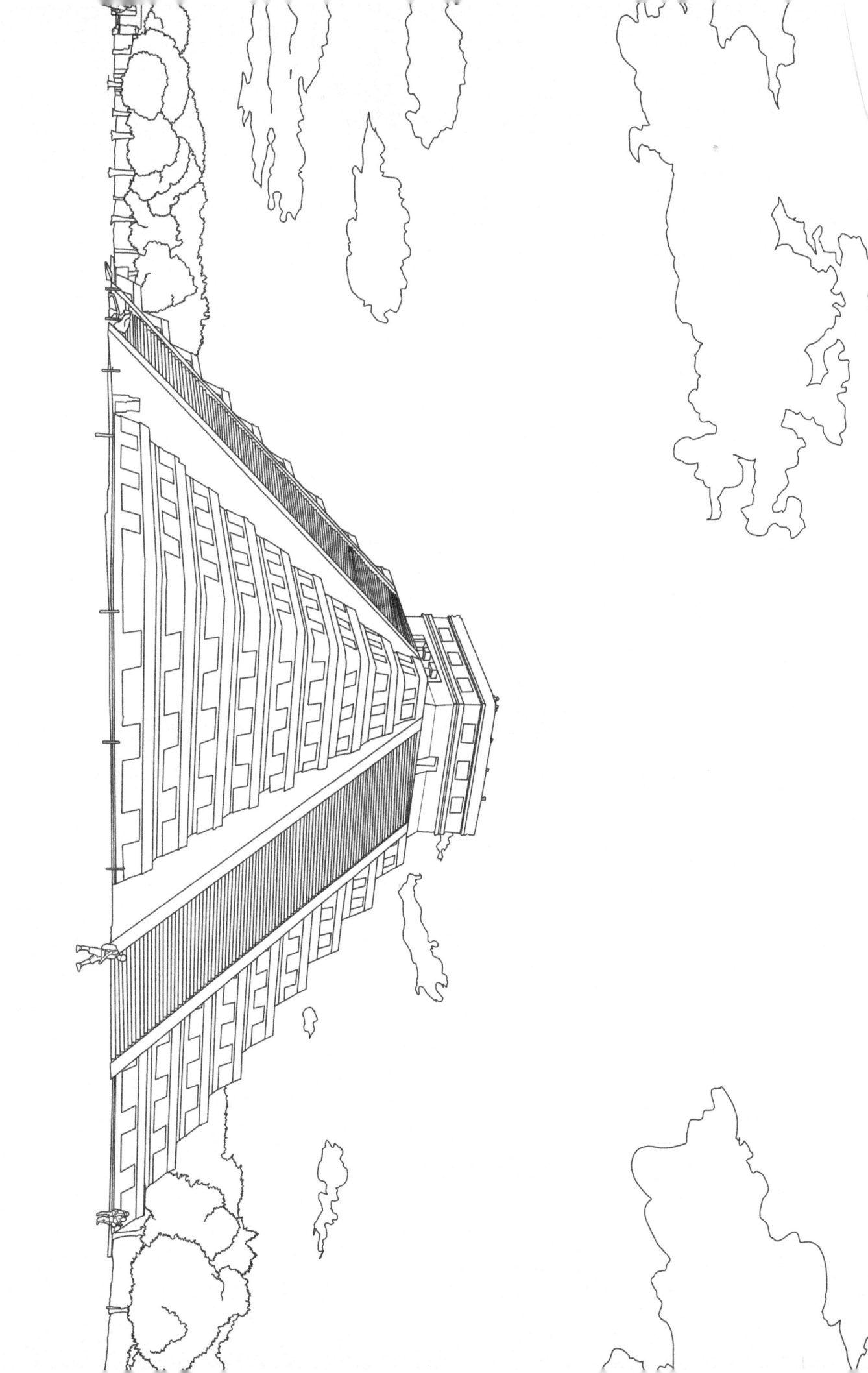

ACROPOLIS

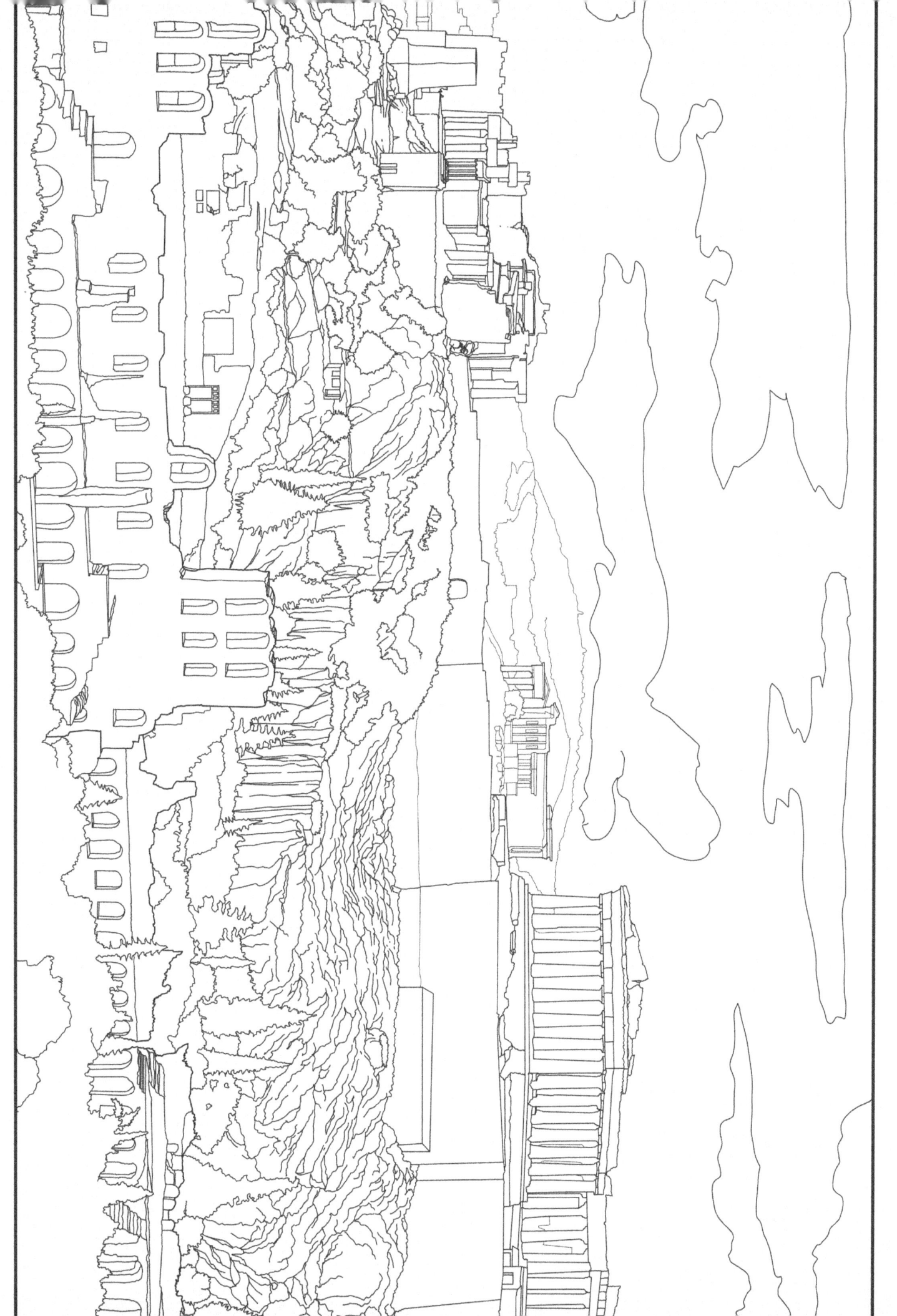